APR 1 4 2008

Dian Fossey

Dian Fossey

AMONG THE GORILLAS

WIL MARA

FRANKLIN WATTS
A Division of Scholastic Inc.
New York Toronto London Auckland Sydney
Mexico City New Delhi Hong Kong
Danbury, Connecticut

For Jenna, Jess, and Lindsey, with all the love in the world.

Photographs © 2004: AP/Wide World Photos: 35, 111; Bob Campbell: front and back cover; Bruce Coleman Inc./Candace Scharsu: 42; Corbis Images: 49, 54, 103, 107 (Yann Arthus-Bertrand), 26 (Bettmann), 25 (Wolfgang Kaehler), 14 (Royalty-Free); Getty Images: 105 (Tyler Hicks), 2 (Neil Selkirk), 23 (Terrence Spencer); Hulton | Archive/Getty Images: 41; Ian Redmond/UNEP/Born Free Foundation: 80, 86, 96; Minden Pictures/ Gerry Ellis: 28, 56, 87; National Geographic Image Collection: 62, 64, 65, 67, 70, 75, 90, 100 (Robert M. Campbell), 74 (Dian Fossey), 47, 112 (Michael Nichols); Peter Arnold Inc.: 58 (Yann Arthus-Bertrand), 79 (Compost/Visage), 44 (Michel Gunther), 30 (Martin Harvey); Ray Pompilio: 98; Stone/Getty Images/Johan Elzenga: 20; The Dian Fossey Gorilla Fund International: 10, 16, 32; The Image Bank/Getty Images/Inc.Archive Holdings: 6.

Library of Congress Cataloging-in-Publication Data

Mara, Wil.
    Dian Fossey : among the gorillas / Wil Mara.
        p. cm. — (Great life stories)
    Summary: Profiles the life of the scientist who studied mountain gorillas in central Africa and worked to ensure their survival.

Includes bibliographical references (p.).

ISBN 0-531-12059-7

1. Fossey, Dian—Juvenile literature. 2.Primatologists—Biography—Juvenile literature. 3. Gorilla—Juvenile literature. [1. Fossey, Dian. 2. Zoologists. 3. Scientists. 4. Gorilla. 5. Women—Biography.] I. Title. II. Series.

QL31.F65M37 2003
599.884'092—dc22

                                                                                                    2003016963

Printed in the United States of America.

1 2 3 4 5 6 7 8 9 10 R 13 12 11 10 09 08 07 06 05 04

Contents

Dian was born during the Great Depression, a time when many Americans struggled to survive after losing their jobs. The people shown here are waiting in line to receive food.

ONE

Early Years

Dian Fossey was born in San Francisco, California, on January 16, 1932. Back in those days, the United States was suffering the many miseries of the Great Depression, a time when millions of people had no jobs and no money. One out of every four people in the country could not find work. Some who had made a good living before the Great Depression now had to beg for money just to buy food to eat. They wore other people's used clothes, and families shared homes with other families because they couldn't afford homes of their own.

Dian's father, George, loved nature and spent as much time out-doors as he could. Because his family needed money to pay the bills and keep food on the table, he worked as an insurance salesman. He didn't like the job, didn't like that kind of life, and soon developed the habit of drinking too much alcohol. He drank to try to forget about how unhappy he was, but his drinking did nothing but get him into trouble.

Dian's mother, Kitty, wasn't pleased with her husband's behavior. She was a stern, proper woman who worried about what other people thought of her. She was a former fashion model who believed that the way others viewed her was tremendously important. If her husband was getting into trouble, her neighbors might hear about it. Then they would talk to other neighbors, and soon the whole town would know what was happening at the Fossey household. She told George he had to get his drinking under control, but he couldn't. He wanted to stop selling insurance, but Kitty wouldn't let him. They were both increasingly unhappy with their relationship and decided to get a divorce. Dian was only three years old at the time. George Fossey went his way, and Kitty Fossey went hers.

The Great Depression

In the 1920s, people were spending money faster than they could make it. They bought things on credit, which means getting whatever they wanted and not paying for the goods until later. While this may have been fun, it was also dangerous. Eventually, people bought too much on credit and could buy no more. That caused a depression, or a time when there was little money in the economy and few jobs available because manufacturers could not sell their goods. Some people lost their homes and had very little food and only the clothes on their backs. This period lasted from 1929 until around the early 1940s. It was one of the saddest times in U.S. history.

Dian lived with her mother, who eventually remarried. Her second husband's name was Richard Price. Kitty took his last name and thus became Kitty Price. Dian, however, kept the name "Fossey." She and her father wrote letters to each other for a while, sometimes exchanging photographs as well. They also made an occasional phone call to each other. Eventually, however, George Fossey faded from Dian's life and then disappeared completely. It wasn't easy keeping him there in the first place. Kitty and Richard did not like Dian to talk about her father. Even mentioning his name might get Dian into trouble.

HARD TIMES AT HOME

Richard was much more like Dian's mother than George had been. He was stern and stiff. He worked very hard, earned a lot of money, and went out of his way to appear respectable and important. He thought children had their place in life, and he wanted to make sure Dian understood that. He punished her if she got into trouble and didn't let her interfere with "adult things" like having other adult friends over for parties or talking with people about important business matters. He believed that adults had their world, and children had theirs, and the two should always be kept separate.

Dian wasn't very happy with any of this, but she made the best of it. She called Richard "Daddy" and tried to do as he asked. She was a naturally friendly, happy person as a youngster, and she got along well with others. While Richard paid for her schooling and took care of her as if she were his own child, he did not have a strong emotional bond with Dian.

While she had a lukewarm relationship with her mother and stepfather, Dian developed a strong connection with animals. Sometimes she even preferred the company of animals to the company of people. She desperately wanted a pet, something she could love and would give her love in return. Her mother and stepfather said no at first, but she kept begging. Eventually, they allowed her to keep a goldfish. Even though it wasn't something she could hug or play with, she was thrilled. Dian worked hard to keep its water clean and do whatever else made the fish happy. Sadly, however, it died one day. She would later say that she cried for a whole week after its death.

By the time Dian was in high school, she had found other animals to love—horses. She was a member of the school's riding club and

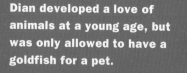
Dian developed a love of animals at a young age, but was only allowed to have a goldfish for a pet.

developed superb skills in everything from trail riding and jumping to basic care and maintenance. When she wasn't working on academics, she could usually be found in the stables. She would lovingly wash and groom the powerful, magnificent creatures, showering them with the affection she couldn't express at home.

FINDING HER WAY

Dian wasn't sure what she wanted to do with her life when the time came for her to go to college. Her mother and stepfather wanted her to try studying business. Dian was fairly sure it wouldn't interest her. However, during her first year at Marin Junior College in 1949, she gave business courses a try. She hated the classes and stopped pretending to like them just to please her parents.

The United States in the 1950s

The late 1940s and the 1950s were a tremendously prosperous time in the United States. World War II ended in 1945, and all the soldiers who had survived it returned home. They found jobs, built homes, and started families. There were exciting scientific advances made at this time as well. More doctors began using a "miracle drug" known as penicillin, which had been discovered only a few decades earlier. It was highly effective in killing disease-causing bacteria. The 1950s also saw the first widespread use of plastic and the birth of the nuclear energy industry.

Dian's experience with horses earned her a job at a ranch in Montana during the summer. She would later call it the best job she ever had. Not only did she get to be with horses all day long, she also got paid for it. The people who worked with her at the Montana ranch would later say it was obvious she loved not just the horses but all the animals she encountered. She seemed to have a magical connection with them.

Once Dian made the decision to reject a career in business, she had to choose a different one. She decided to become a veterinarian. In 1950, she enrolled in the University of California at Davis and began taking the appropriate courses. She excelled at the basic subjects, such as botany and zoology, but she was also required to master more difficult subjects, such as organic chemistry and animal anatomy. These advanced topics baffled her. She tried her best, but she just couldn't understand them. By her second year, her dreams of becoming a veterinarian were gone. She failed out of school. It was time yet again for her to choose a different career path.

TWO

Moving Out of California

Fossey decided to work with children with disabilities. Some of these disabilities were emotional, and others were physical. If a child was sick, she wanted to help. She enrolled in San Jose State College and worked hard. In 1954, she graduated with a degree in occupational therapy. Less than a year after graduation, she found a job at a children's hospital in Louisville, Kentucky. It was an administrative position, which meant it required her not only to work with the children who were patients there, but also to manage a small staff.

Not long after Fossey began working at the hospital she found a place to live—a small cottage on a farm a few miles away from Louisville.

It was old and run-down, but she loved it. She had lived in or near cities all her life and had never liked them. The country, with its green pastures and quiet streams, felt more like home to her. She spent hours staring

Fossey made her third attempt at earning a college degree at San Jose State College. This time she studied occupational therapy, which led to a job at a children's hospital.

out the cottage windows, admiring the blazing reds and yellows of the autumn trees and the numerous animals that ran free. Now that she was away from California and her parents, she was happier than ever. She would rarely go back to California for the rest of her life.

THE HENRY FAMILY

While Fossey was living in Kentucky, she met a woman who would change her life. The woman's name was Mary White Henry. Henry also worked at the children's hospital. She could see that Fossey was unsure about how to fit into her new Kentucky world, so she took the shy California girl around the city at night, introducing her to people she knew. Some of these people were men who did not have wives or girl-friends. A few of them found Fossey attractive and wanted to get to know her better. One even asked her to marry him, but Fossey turned down the offer. In her heart, she knew her one true love in life was animals. It would be unfair to marry someone. She would remain unmarried her whole life.

Another group of people that Mary White Henry introduced to Fossey was her family. Mary's mother, in particular, whose name was Gaynee Henry, would have an effect on Fossey like no other person. Gaynee Henry was small and beautiful, and she had a great love for everyone she met. She was gentle and kind and could make people feel wonderful about themselves. Because Fossey's own mother could be so cold and unpleasant, Fossey developed a deep fondness for Gaynee. After a night out with Mary, Fossey would often go back to Gaynee's house and spend hours talking with her. Soon Mary was joking that Fossey was one of her mother's other daughters.

One thing Fossey found fascinating about Gaynee was her deep devotion to religion. Gaynee was a devout Catholic. Every night, she would pray and ask God for strength and guidance. Gaynee had suffered some horrible losses in her life—her husband and two of her children

Fossey spends her time with some of her patients at the hospital. She became good friends with one of her coworkers, Mary White Henry.

had died—and she felt that her love for God helped her get through these tragedies.

Gaynee enjoyed having people in her home. Fossey was amazed to see all sorts of friends and relatives coming and going at all hours. They came in, sat down, shared a meal, and talked and joked as if they lived there. Gaynee's home became known as the "Henry Hotel." It was very different from the household of Fossey's parents back in California. One person who often visited the Henry Hotel was a man named Father Raymond, a Catholic priest. Fossey found him interesting because he was incredibly smart and had ideas about many subjects. He could talk for hours about the strangest things and had an enthusiasm that Fossey found exciting. She would ask him questions about God that had weighed on her mind for years, and he would give her answers she found satisfying. She would also talk with him about life in general, and through his kindness and intelligence he would give her ideas that she adopted as her own. He would tell her about the Catholic Church, about its practices, and how he felt strongly about them. She was very impressed with him.

FOSSEY FINDS RELIGION

After her long conversations with both Gaynee and Father Raymond, Fossey decided that she, too, wanted to become a member of the Catholic Church. After she joined, she wrote a letter to her mother and told her about it. Instead of being happy, her mother was upset. She thought Fossey should have talked it over with her first. Fossey didn't care. She decided to devote her life to caring for others and trying to make the world a better place. By putting other people's interests before her own, she felt as if she were moving farther away from her parents' way of life. In her eyes, all they cared about was themselves. She never wanted to be like that.

When Fossey wasn't working at the hospital, she was working on improving herself. She took music lessons and creative writing courses. She didn't like to waste time on things that didn't make her a better person. She spent almost no time at all watching television or relaxing. She had a huge supply of energy, and she spent it on things she considered productive. In some ways, this suggested that she still hadn't found her true focus in life. However, that would soon change.

THREE

African Fever

Mary White Henry traveled as often as she could. She had been to Europe and Asia more than once by the time she met Fossey. In 1960, she traveled to Africa. The trip normally would have been very expensive, but she worked for a travel agency at the time and could get good deals on airfare and hotel rooms. She also had friends there. These friends brought her to some of the continent's most intriguing and exotic places. One time she went to the wilds of Rhodesia, known today as Zimbabwe, which is a land of lush greenery and majestic mountains, where giant hippopotamuses bathe in broad rivers and giraffes meander through waving grasslands. When Henry came home, she had plenty of stories to tell and had plenty of photographs to show.

Henry's family was interested in hearing about her trip and seeing her pictures, but it was Fossey who was most captivated by the stories. She couldn't believe the beauty of the faraway world she saw in those

The stories and photographs of Mary White Henry's travels in Africa captivated Fossey. She wanted to see the continent with all of its striking scenery and exotic wildlife.

photographs. She was also hypnotized by the stories. It didn't take long for her to decide that she had to visit Africa some day. She had to see it for herself—the wild green forests, the churning rivers, and the thousands of exotic animals that she would never encounter in the United States. In the United States, there were few untouched stretches of nature. In Africa, however, there were millions of acres of land that had not yet been developed by humans.

The problem, Fossey knew right from the start, was that, unlike Mary Henry, she didn't have the money to go on such a trip. She didn't earn much money working at the children's hospital, so she would have trouble paying for the trip. When she looked into the cost of a basic trip to Africa, she discovered it would be about as much money as she earned in a whole year at the hospital! She couldn't imagine how she would possibly cover the expenses. Her parents had more than enough money to send her, but she did not want to ask a favor of them.

Africa in the 1960s

The African continent was undergoing tremendous political changes when Mary White Henry visited in 1960. Before World War II, many of its countries were controlled by European nations such as England, France, and Belguim. After the war, however, those nations were weakened from the fighting, and many native African people saw the chance to break away from them and gain independence. In 1960 alone, seventeen African nations declared themselves free of European rule. Then they focused on learning how to govern themselves.

So Fossey set this dream aside, and a few more years passed. She was still living in Kentucky, still working at the hospital, and still wishing she could travel to Africa. Her life was going nowhere, and she knew it. She was a naturally restless person, eager to grow and develop. She decided that, one way or another, she was going to make it to Africa by the end of 1963.

Fossey finally decided to take out a loan. She broke down and asked her parents to lend her the money. At first they agreed, but then they changed their minds. They felt the trip was too dangerous and foolish. So Fossey went to a savings and loans bank. A bank official said the bank would give Fossey the money she needed, but only at an interest rate of nearly 18 percent. That meant whatever amount of money she took from the loan company, she had to pay that same amount back, plus 18 percent. She hoped to make the money back by writing articles and taking pictures of the trip and then selling them to magazines or newspapers.

PREPARING FOR THE BEST

Fossey took her time getting ready. She read everything she could about Africa. She talked to others who'd gone there, hoping to get some idea of what to expect and where to go. She planned a packed schedule so every moment would be productive. She bought some of the basic things she would need—boots, a new jacket, medicine, soap, and other supplies. She decided to stay in nice hotels so she could shower and get plenty of rest each night. She also got treated for her allergies, of which she had many. It was common for an American visiting Africa to get sick. There were lots of viruses and bacteria common there that an

American's body was not used to. She wanted to make sure she got the shots she needed to protect herself.

During her research, she came across a book called *The Year of the Gorilla*. It was written by a man named George Schaller, and it was about the year Schaller spent in Africa studying the gorillas that lived in the Virunga Mountains. Schaller wrote that these beautiful animals were not violent toward humans, which is how they had always been regarded. They were vegetarians and lived quiet, peaceful lives. Fossey was so dazzled by Schaller's book that she decided to extend her trip by a few weeks just so she could visit the Virunga Mountains and—she hoped—see some of the gorillas he'd written about.

Fossey left for Africa on September 26, 1963. Africa is the second largest continent in the world, comprised of more than 30 million square miles (48,280,320 square kilometers). It is home to nearly 800 million people, which is more than three times the number of people who live in the United

George Schaller's study of gorillas in the Virunga Mountains inspired Fossey to visit the area.

States. Africa contains more than fifty countries. Most of the land is flat, but there are a few majestic mountain ranges and broad river valleys. Africa is also home to the Sahara, the largest desert in the world. Africa contains every type of environment imaginable, from open grasslands and rolling prairies to lush tropical rain forests.

Fossey decided to begin her trip in Kenya, which is located on Africa's eastern coast. She flew into Nairobi, Kenya's capital. One of her first goals was to find a guide—someone who knew the area well and could bring her wherever she wanted to go. She ended up hiring a man named John Alexander, who had been a professional guide in Africa for years. Alexander told her they should take a route he called the "milk run." It was a thousand-mile stretch of rugged roads that would allow Fossey to see all of the area's most beautiful environments and amazing creatures. She would finally get to see elephants, rhinoceroses, lions, and gazelles up close.

THE MAN WHO WOULD CHANGE HER LIFE

While on this journey, Alexander suggested they go to a place called Olduvai Gorge, Tanzania, in the hopes of seeing a husband-and-wife scientist team named the Leakeys. Olduvai Gorge was basically a gigantic hole—295 feet (90 meters) deep and about 30 miles (48.2 kilometers) long—in the African land that had been created by an earthquake. Inside the gorge were fossils that shed light on the evolution of human beings. The Leakeys, Louis and Mary, first discovered them in the 1940s. By the time Fossey visited Africa, the Leakeys were famous around the world for their work in the gorge. However, in spite of their fame, they did not give interviews and resented having their work interrupted by visits from outsiders.

When Fossey finally met the Leakeys, she went out of her way to assure them that she was not a reporter from a magazine or a newspaper. Because the Leakeys were so well known for their desire to be left alone,

Scientists have found many fossils in Olduvai Gorge. The fossils help scientists better understand the types of plant and animal life that existed long ago.

The Leakeys

Louis and Mary Leakey devoted years of hard work to uncovering answers to the mystery of human evolution. In 1959, Mary Leakey discovered a skull that appeared to be a clear link in evolution between humans and apes. A few years later, she and Louis made a second significant fossil find that demonstrated not only another human–ape link. The discovery also suggested that the humanlike animal made and used tools. The popular journal *National Geographic* ran many articles and photos on their work, and the Leakeys published numerous books and articles of their own.

Fossey was afraid they'd be somewhat grumpy with her, maybe even a little nasty. She was pleasantly surprised to find them to be friendly. She told them she came to Africa to study the same gorillas George Schaller wrote about in his book, and she didn't try to hide the fact that she was not a professional scientist. Louis Leakey told her he was sure gorillas were a key part of human evolution and encouraged her to follow her dream of studying them. This show of support strengthened Fossey's determination. It also was not the last time she would see the Leakeys.

It is interesting to note that no one in Fossey's life up to this point seems to remember her mentioning an interest in the gorillas of the Virunga Mountains. Even her good friend Mary White Henry, whom Fossey told many things, does not recall ever having a conversation about them. Either it was an ambition that Fossey kept to herself for many years, or she was so inspired by George Schaller's book during her preparation for the trip that it changed the focus of her entire life. No one will ever know for sure.

FOSSEY'S FIRST CONTACT

A few days after the meeting the Leakeys, Fossey and her guide stopped at a hotel called the Travellers Rest. It was located on the western side of the Virunga Mountains and was run by a man named Walter Baumgärtel. Baumgärtel was a large, jolly individual who loved having people around. He had been in charge of the Travellers Rest for years and had hundreds of stories to tell about the gorillas. Countless people had come to the hotel to see them, including many well-known scientists. Few people knew more about them and their ways than Baumgärtel did.

He told Fossey and her guide that they should go to a place called Mount Mikeno, which was about a day away by truck. There they would find a pair of wildlife photographers named Alan and Joan Root. They were in the area for the same reason as Fossey—to see the gorillas. Fossey decided to take Baumgärtel's advice.

The problem was that she and her guide had to climb Mount Mikeno to get to the Roots' camp, and Mikeno was 14,557 feet (4,437 m) high. Fossey had always been a very determined person, ready to face whatever challenges life put in front of her, but even she had no idea what this would be like. First of all, she and her guide had loads of supplies—medicine, clothing, camera equipment, and other items. It all had to be taken along. They figured out quickly that they wouldn't be able to carry it all. They would have to hire some help. In the end, they brought more than a dozen extra people along. Another problem was the hike

Climbing Mount Mikeno was a great physical challenge for Fossey. The journey took her approximately six hours.

itself—it was very steep and rocky. Sometimes Fossey had to hold onto branches and vines to keep from falling. There was also the thin air—the higher they climbed, the thinner the air became and the harder it was to breathe. By the time Fossey got to the camp more than six hours later, she felt like she was going to pass out. She wrote, "My rib cage was bursting, my legs were creaking in agony, and my ankle felt as though a crocodile had his jaws around it."

The Roots were a lot like the Leakeys—they were very involved in their work and did not like to be interrupted. At first, they didn't feel any differently toward Fossey and her group, but eventually they became friendlier. When they asked her to join them on a hike in the hope of seeing some gorillas, Fossey jumped at the chance. It was a decision that would change her life.

They moved through the dense jungle slowly and carefully, their senses sharp and alert. The Roots moved along quickly and easily, having been there many times before. Fossey had a much harder time, but her excitement was so great that she managed to keep up. Before she saw any of the gorillas, she smelled them. There was a heavy, musky animal scent in the air that Fossey found unpleasant and fascinating at the same time. It certainly was an odor she had never encountered before. Then came the sounds—high-pitched screaming that shocked her like the poke of a stick. There were thick leaves and vines all around, making it impossible to see anything. One of the African guides cut a hole in the green wall, and suddenly, just like that, there they were—a small group of half a dozen gorillas, as amazed to see humans as the humans were to see them.

Fossey would later say that they did not look cruel or evil, as so many people had reported through the years. She said they looked gentle,

With the help of a guide, Fossey was able to get her first glimpse of mountain gorillas.

curious, and even a little frightened. She also thought they were among the most beautiful animals she had ever seen. Deep down, she sensed that she would be seeing them again.

Meet the Mountain Gorilla

Mountain gorillas are found only in mountainous regions of Africa. Mature males are called silverbacks, while younger males are called blackbacks. All mountain gorillas are herbivorous, which means they eat only plant matter, such as fruits, leaves, stems, and roots. They build camps in which to sleep in a different location every night. The females and the young often sleep in trees, whereas the males remain on the ground in case of trouble. Like humans, the females give birth to only one baby at a time. The average life span of a mountain gorilla is about thirty-five years. They are an endangered species because their habitat has been decimated by human development, especially over the last fifty years.

Fossey finished her travels with a visit to friends of Mary White Henry.

FOUR

Returning to the "Real World"

Not long after the gorilla sighting, Fossey's African adventure was over. She returned to the hotel, where she got a good night's rest. The next day she visited some of Mary White Henry's friends, the Forresters, who lived on a farm near the city of Victoria. While there, she met one of the Forrester sons, Alexie, and was swept off her feet. "He's thirty-one, single, and just about the best-looking man I've ever laid eyes on," she would write later. In the years to come they would have an on-again, off-again relationship that almost ended in marriage, but did not because of Fossey's eventual devotion to the gorillas she loved so much. After her visit with the Forresters, Fossey returned to Kentucky and to her job at the children's hospital. She now had to pay off the huge loan she'd taken out to pay for the trip. So, as she had planned, she began writing articles that she hoped to sell. She also went through the hundreds of photographs she took, hoping to sell those too. She even tried writing a novel for children, but the first publisher to read it asked for so many changes that she became discouraged and gave up.

Eventually, she sold an article and some pictures to Louisville's *Courier Journal*. She also went back to spending time with Mary Henry and going out at night. In many ways, her life returned to normal, which worried her. She was afraid it would stay that way forever unless something interesting happened. As it turned out, that something was just around the corner.

THE OPPORTUNITY OF A LIFETIME

In March of 1966, Louis Leakey came to Louisville. He was on a lecture tour, talking to large groups of people about his findings in Olduvai Gorge. After his Louisville talk, Fossey went up to him. She wasn't sure if he would even remember her—being so famous, he met many new people every day—but he did. "When my turn came," she later wrote, "he gave me a crinkly smile of recognition and gave my hand a good long squeeze. I was so surprised he knew me." In fact, when he saw her, he began asking questions about her trip—the things she saw, whether she was still interested in studying gorillas, and what her plans were for the future.

Fossey told Leakey that she was still very much interested in studying the gorillas she had seen in the Virunga Mountains, and that she had no definite plans for the future. Leakey then shocked her by saying he felt she was the perfect person to undertake a huge project he was planning—for one person to go back to Africa and conduct long-term research on gorillas in the hopes that learning about them would shed more light on the evolution of human beings.

Fossey was speechless. Surely, she thought, this either must be a very detailed dream or an enormous practical joke. "It's not possible," she wrote. "Things just don't happen like this!" She reminded Leakey that

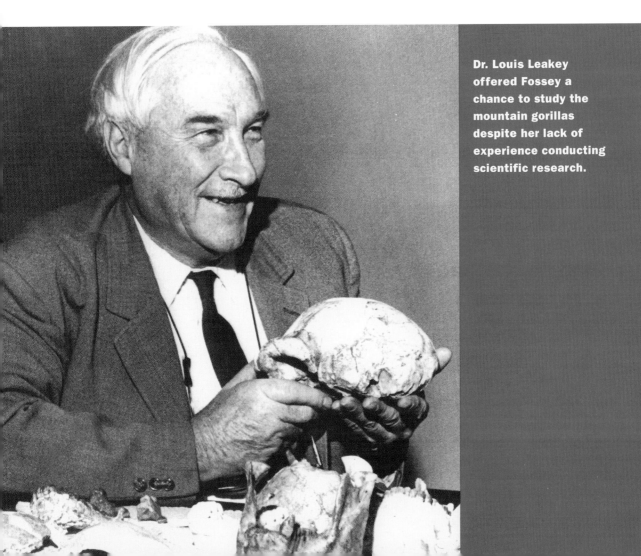

Dr. Louis Leakey offered Fossey a chance to study the mountain gorillas despite her lack of experience conducting scientific research.

she had no formal training in the sciences, so she didn't feel qualified to handle such a huge responsibility. Leakey said that was okay—he wanted someone "fresh," not someone who was "overtrained." Fossey then pointed out that she had no money for such a project, and even if she did, she still had to pay off the last African trip. Leakey said that, too, was okay. He was sure he could raise enough money to pay all her expenses, plus perhaps even give her some extra money for herself. It was clear that Leakey was determined to have Fossey undertake this project.

Something else unusual happened during this meeting. Leakey asked Fossey if she still had her appendix. The appendix is an organ in the human body. It is part of the large intestine and is believed to be generally useless. At the time, many people had theirs removed when they were young to avoid the risk of developing two dangerous conditions later in life—appendicitis and peritonitis.

Fossey told Leakey that she still had hers, and Leakey suggested that she have it removed. If it burst while she was in the middle of the African jungle, no one would be able to help her, and she might die. So, eager to please Dr. Leakey and to be as prepared for the trip as possible,

A Nation at War

In 1966, the United States was fighting a war against the Asian nation of North Vietnam. The president at the time was Lyndon Baines Johnson, and the war was not popular at home. Thousands of Americans, most of them very young, actively protested U.S. involvement in the war by marching in the streets and refusing the join the military.

she had the operation. Ironically, Leakey wrote a letter afterwards stating that he didn't think it was necessary for her to have it removed after all.

LEAVING THE UNITED STATES BEHIND

Fossey was thrilled about the trip, even if it meant leaving Louisville behind. She had grown close to so many people. Now she had to say goodbye to them, and she wasn't sure how long it would be before she would see them again. She resigned her position at the children's hospital, packed her things, and went to California to visit her parents one last time.

They were not happy about her decision to accept Leakey's offer. Her stepfather thought it was pure foolishness, and her mother was so upset she could barely speak. They both wondered why Fossey couldn't find a nice young man to marry, buy a home, and start having children. Fossey told them she wanted different things from life. Perhaps Africa wouldn't hold the key to her happiness after all, but she was certainly going to find out. She left without their blessings.

Her parents weren't the only ones who thought the idea was foolish. Many people in the scientific community who knew Leakey thought he had lost his mind. They wondered why a brilliant scientist would choose an inexperienced person to undertake such an important project—very much the same question Fossey had asked him during their last meeting. Leakey, however, stood by his decision, assuring everyone that Fossey would grow into the job and do very well. Fossey sometimes thought Leakey had more confidence in her than she had in herself.

FIVE

A Tropical Paradise

Fossey left for Africa on December 15, 1966. Because she would be staying so much longer than she had on the first trip, she brought along even more luggage. She took enough clothing to last for years, along with basic medical supplies in case of an emergency, and enough pencils, pens, pads, and typewriter ribbons to equip a small office. She would have to write a few books and articles while there. This was part of the deal with Dr. Leakey and the people who were paying for the project. She also brought hundreds of rolls of film for her camera. Dr. Leakey expected her to take literally thousands of color pictures of anything and everything relating to the gorillas. She would document where they slept, what they ate, how they behaved, and the areas in which they lived. The books and articles she would publish, he knew, would be greatly enhanced by these amazing images. She would also give lectures in years to come, and she would dazzle audiences with the photographs.

Christmas was coming up fast when Fossey arrived, and Leakey asked her to spend it with Jane Goodall and her husband. Goodall was studying chimpanzees at Lake Baringo and, like Fossey, had been hand-picked and funded by Leakey. Leakey wanted Fossey to see Goodall's camp—how it was set up, how Goodall ran her day-to-day life, and how she conducted her research. One funny incident occurred during this visit. One of Goodall's chimpanzees became frightened by the sight of a leopard-skin bag Fossey brought along and ran screaming into the jungle.

A few days later, Fossey was back in the Virunga Mountains. She stopped to visit her old friend Walter Baumgärtel, who was glad to see her and excited about the project. Then she and her group went back up the same mountain trail she'd climbed during the first trip. Fossey recognized some of the same trees and shrubs. The beauty of the area was still so amazing to her—the long mountain range, the lush green leaves, the sounds of the wild animals. She was both amazed and pleased to see that almost nothing had changed in the years since she'd last been there.

HOME SWEET HOME

When the group finally reached the spot where the camp would be set up, they quickly went to work. One of the people helping Fossey was Alan Root, the photographer she met during the last trip. He and the others could only stay for a few days, so they had to get everything arranged fast. Eventually the camp was built and ready, and the group

Jane Goodall's Work

Jane Goodall spent nearly ten years studying chimpanzees in Africa, beginning in 1960 on the shores of the famous Lake Tanganyika. During this time, she made some groundbreaking discoveries about chimpanzee behavior. For example, she noted that they use grass "tubes" to suck termites out of small holes. She also realized that chimpanzees exhibit certain affectionate gestures that humans do, including hugs, kisses, and pats on the back. She wrote a very popular book about chimpanzees called *In the Shadow of Man*, which was published in 1971. In 1977, she set up the Goodall Institute for Wildlife Research, Education, and Conservation. She has also set up sanctuaries for sick and orphaned chimpanzees in several African countries.

went on their way. Suddenly Fossey was alone. She would later say that watching the others leave was one of the most difficult things she ever had to do. The loneliness that followed was almost too much to bear.

Fossey was delighted to return to the Virunga Mountains and looked forward to starting her work with the mountain gorillas.

She wouldn't be alone for long—four days later a man named Sanwekwe arrived. He was an African native and one of the best animal trackers in the world. If anyone could find gorillas, he could. Fossey met him during her first trip, and he had also helped George Schaller, the man who wrote the book on gorillas that Fossey liked so much.

Not wanting to waste any time, Fossey ventured into the forest with Sanwekwe right away. During this first journey, they found a single male gorilla that, upon seeing them, became quite angry and ran off. A few hours later, they found another one that was a lot calmer and more relaxed. From a safe distance, Fossey began scribbling notes about everything she felt was important—what the gorilla was doing, where it was sitting, the time of day, and so on. She noted that it began beating its chest and making soft "hoots." Then a few more gorillas arrived. There is little doubt that they were surprised to see this woman standing in the middle of their forest, but they showed no aggression toward her.

When Fossey got back to camp that night, she sat at her typewriter and began typing her notes about everything she'd seen and experienced. She would continue typing these notes at the end of each day, and in time, she would have thousands of pages. Her notes not only helped her write all her books and articles later on, they also documented new information on the lives of gorillas. For example, Fossey realized that the gorilla groups she was observing weren't just a bunch of random specimens, but in fact were very structured family groups. The group consisted of one main adult male called the silverback, a few younger males, several adult females, and the children. The silverback would act as the protector of the group, fending off other animals that might threaten the females or the younger and weaker children. The

During the day, Fossey observed the gorillas and made careful notes of their activities.

silverback remained the leader of each family group until he either died or became too old to perform his duties. At that time, a new male within the group took over. Fossey also saw the males in each group take care of the young just as the females did, handling them gently and with great affection. All of this behavioral information was previously unknown. So, even thought she wasn't officially a scientist, Fossey was making important contributions to the scientific world.

In time, Fossey discovered that she could gain more trust from the gorillas and get them to relax when they saw her if she imitated some of their actions and sounds. She would crouch down the way a gorilla would crouch, chew on the same vegetables, try to make the same noises, beat her chest, or scratch her head. She wrote in her notes that she felt silly at times and that she would never act in such a way if there were other people around. Strangely enough, however, her willingness to act foolishly helped her study the animals more closely.

After a while, she became familiar with the individual gorillas who lived nearby. There were only a few hundred, and Fossey began to recognize each one by certain physical characteristics. Soon, she began giving them names. One of the first to get a name was No-Nose, an old female who looked as though she had no nose because the one she had was so flat and small. Other early names included Popcorn, Tagalong, and Cassius. Each name held some meaning, in some cases a meaning that only Fossey understood.

Even though Fossey was not, as she had said many times, officially trained in any of the areas of science that studied animals, such as zoology, ecology, conservation, and behavioralism—she became very good at spotting signs of gorillas in the forest. She could tell if a gorilla group had been in a certain area by studying broken branches or knuckle-prints on the ground or in the grass. Sometimes the gorillas would tear bark from trees or pull down vines. The forest may have seemed like a confused, tangled mass to her when she first arrived, but after a time, it all began making sense.

Only about two months after she arrived in Africa, she heard from the people at *National Geographic*. *National Geographic* is the publication of the National Geographic Society, whose goal is to spread information about interesting places around the world. The magazine's primary topics include archaeology, geography, and biology, and it features superbly written articles and breathtaking photographs. The society often gives money to scientists working on particularly interesting projects, and it is a great honor for a writer or photographer to have his or her work appear in the magazine. In Fossey's case, the magazine's editors wanted some material concerning the gorillas. They even mentioned sending a film crew to the Virunga Mountains so it could make a television documentary. Fossey was thrilled by all of this.

UPS AND DOWNS OF JUNGLE LIVING

Soon after this exciting news, Fossey had her first bad experience with poachers. Poachers are people who take plants and animals out of the wild in order to make money. They often trap the animals and sell them live or kill them and sell their fur or other parts of their bodies. Fossey knew there were poachers in the area where she was studying the gorillas, and she knew the gorillas were sometimes what the poachers were after, but she had not yet encountered a major poaching problem.

Conflict at Home

Back in the United States, the country experienced a great amount of violence in 1967. First, many people were protesting against U.S. involvement in the war in Vietnam. The U.S. government wanted to recruit as many young people as possible to help with the fight, but thousands refused and took to the streets, carrying signs that advocated peace and freedom. There were also many "race riots"—fighting and killing that took place largely in the nation's inner cities—driven by decades of simmering anger between minorities who wanted a better life, and the whites who strove to keep it from them. Some of America's youth soon declared the summer of 1967 as the "Summer of Love" in an effort combat the anger, hatred, and destruction.

Then, one day while she was out with Sanwekwe, she came across a group of poachers. She took their weapons away and then she and Sanwekwe tried to bring them to the people who protected the area so they could be arrested. The problem was that the poachers were born and raised in the Virunga Mountains and knew the area better than anyone, better than even Sanwekwe himself. They began disappearing into the dense forest one at a time, and soon they were all gone. It was a frustrating experience for Fossey, and it would not be the last. She would have many unpleasant encounters with poachers in the years ahead.

She was getting used to her new life in the mountains, but there were still problems. She needed decent food, and that often meant having to take a long trip into the nearby village of Kibumba. She tried growing

Snares, such as this one shown here, were used by poachers to trap gorillas.

vegetables, but they kept getting smashed by wild animals. She bought a hen and a rooster, and the hen sometimes laid eggs.

Getting mail was also a bit of a hassle. She had to drive a few hours to see her friend Walter Baumgärtel. Baumgärtel allowed her to have all of her mail sent to his hotel.

Another problem was caused by some of the people who were helping her at the campsite. They all lived in the area and were friendly to Fossey when she first arrived. After a while, however, they became rude and difficult. They would often ignore her when she asked them to do something, and in some cases they interfered with her study of the gorillas. In the end, she had to be tough with them so they knew she was in charge. This worked—their attitudes soon changed—but Fossey didn't like being stern. She felt like she was being forced into it.

In spite of all these obstacles, Fossey was excited about seeing the gorillas every day and happy to be doing something she truly loved. She felt the rewards far outweighed the troubles. She wasn't living the most glamorous life, but, in her mind, it was the most interesting. She decorated some of the rooms in her hut to give them a more personal touch, which made her feel good. She felt like she was making her own little place within this strange tropical world.

One of the brightest moments in these early months came when two gorillas from a larger group she was watching came within 20 feet (6.1 m) of her and stayed there for more than an hour. All the gorillas in the group knew she was there, but, obviously, they had begun to become used to seeing her and—perhaps most importantly—began to trust her. They knew she wasn't going to hurt them, so they just went about their business. Fossey would later write that this was one of the greatest days of her life. She wrote many pages about it that night and wrote letters to her friends and family that everything was going wonderfully. At last, the project seemed to be moving along.

Then it all changed.

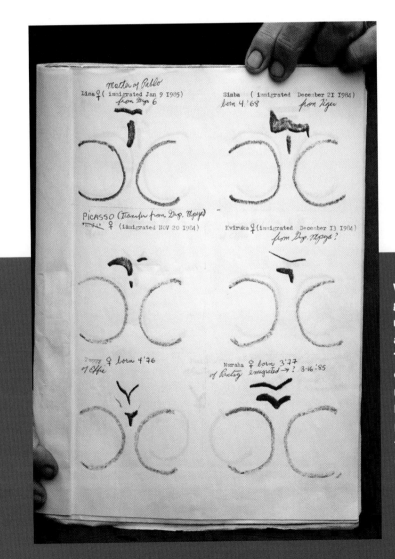

While studying the gorillas, Fossey noted many different things about the gorillas. This is a page from one of Fossey's later notebooks, showing her sketches of the pattern of ridges and furrows on the faces of several gorillas.

SIX

Paradise Lost

Dian Fossey came back to her campsite from a day in the forest to find a group of soldiers waiting for her. This was in July of 1967, just six months after she'd arrived in Africa. The soldiers told her she had to pack up everything and leave at once. Fossey demanded an explanation. She was told that battles had erupted in the area and that she was in tremendous danger. Many innocent people had already been killed, the soldiers said.

The fighting was raging between the military of the existing Congolese government, led by President Joseph Désiré Mobutu, and rebel forces led by a Belgian mercenary named Jean Schramme. Schramme's army wanted to take Mobutu out of power and replace him with a man named Moise Tshombe, who had been the Congo's leader years earlier but had been removed from power by Mobutu through the use of military force. This kind of exchange of power is called a coup.

Fossey knew the area had a lot of problems with fighting before she even got there. In spite of all this, she was still furious about the disruption. She didn't care that fighting was going on. She felt she wasn't a part of it and didn't really care what either side was fighting for. All she wanted to do was study her gorillas and be left alone. The soldiers, however, wouldn't listen to her. They were trying to protect her and had been ordered to get her out of there.

The Long and Painful Saga of the Congo

Life in the Congo has never been easy. Its people fell under the control of the nation of Portugal in the late 1400s. Many of the Congolese people became victims of the slave trade and were taken from their homes and sold abroad. In the late 1800s, Belgium claimed control of the area, which was then called the "Belgian Congo." Life for the native Congolese people improved slightly under Belgian rule, but the people wanted to run their country on their own. They declared themselves a free nation in June of 1960. An internal power struggle began as warring factions fought for control of the country. This power struggle was still raging when Dian Fossey set up her first camp in late 1966. To this day, the newly named Democratic Republic of the Congo does not have a stable government.

LETTING GO AND MOVING ON

With tears in her eyes, Fossey packed up everything of importance, loaded it into her truck, and drove away from the paradise she had come to love so much. She got to see all the women and children in the village of Kibumba come out to say goodbye to her. She promised them she'd be back because she couldn't bear the thought of never seeing the gorillas again. They weren't just animals she was studying for scientific research anymore. They were her family.

Fossey ended up at Walter Baumgärtel's hotel. She was angrier than she'd ever been in her life and wanted to know when she could go back to the campsite. When that answer finally came, she was speechless—two to four months at the earliest. That was far too long for Fossey to wait. She knew that one of the keys to studying the gorillas was observing them every day.

She went to Nairobi, the capital of Kenya, to discuss the situation with Louis Leakey. She would later say that she was terrified about this meeting. She was sure Leakey would be furious that she had allowed her work to be interrupted. She knew he had been in similar situations and had somehow managed to keep working. She expected him to be so disappointed that he would cancel the project on the spot and send her back to the United States.

Instead, Leakey greeted her with a smile and a hug, and told her that he was concerned first and foremost with her safety. He told her there was a need to study gorillas in other parts of Africa, and that someone also needed to study orangutans in the country of Borneo. She was welcome to take part in either of those projects if she wished. She politely turned down the offers, however, saying she was determined to stay with the gorillas of the Virunga Mountains. She would have to study them from a different place, but she would not leave them. Leakey admired her for this determination.

After being forced to leave her research station in the Congo, Fossey met with Louis Leakey in Nairobi to discuss the future.

HOME SWEET HOME, PART II

Fossey set out to find a place where she could still find gorillas, but where there was no fighting. She went to the nation of Rwanda and stayed at the home of a woman named Alyette DeMunck. DeMunck was a new friend who lived at the base of Mount Karisimbi. Karisimbi was part of the Virunga Mountain chain. Because of this, it had the same habitat as the place where Fossey set up her first camp. Fossey hoped to find gorillas there.

Fossey didn't see any gorillas during the first trip through the Karisimbi forest. On the second day, however, her spirits skyrocketed. She not only came across a group of gorillas, she came across a group she knew. Almost five months had passed since she last saw them, and she was relieved to find that they all seemed to be in good health. One of them even had had a baby.

Rwanda in the Late 1960s

Rwanda, like many African nations suddenly faced with the responsibility of political independence, was going through a period of political turmoil. There were two leading groups at the time—the Hutus and the Tutsis. While under European rule, the Tutsis were given more privileges and better educations than were the Hutus. In 1959, the Hutus rebelled, and thousands of Tutsis fled to the neighboring nation of Burundi. By the early 1960s the Hutus ran Rwanda without input from the European powers and elected a president, Gregoire Kayibanda. Fighting between Hutus and Tutsis continued. In the late 1960s, thousands of Tutsis were either killed or fled to Burundi.

Now that she knew where to find the gorillas, she had to set up a second camp. She climbed to the upper reaches of Karisimbi and, with binoculars in hand, searched the area for the perfect site. She decided on what appeared to be a quiet spot that lay between Karisimbi and a mountain next to it called Visoke.

She and DeMunck packed all of Fossey's things and got on the road. They weren't sure exactly where to set up the new camp, but Fossey figured she'd know the right place when she saw it. Along with DeMunck, she was also accompanied by a small team of native Rwandans, who knew the area much better than she did. She saw a few spots she liked, but the natives told her they knew of one that was better. Fossey trusted them, and she was glad she did. They led her to a sunny, grassy meadow with a cool stream flowing through it. The moment she saw it, she decided it was one of the most beautiful places on Earth.

Fossey decided to try to study the mountain gorillas in another part of the Virunga Mountains. This time she would work near Mount Karisimbi.

SEVEN

Paradise Regained— Karisoke

Because this site was located between Karisimbi and Visoke Mountains, Fossey decided to combine the two names and call it Karisoke. She even wrote down the time and date she got there—4:30 P.M. on September 24, 1967. She set up a tent for the time being. Once she settled in and established a routine again, she would go about building a more permanent home.

ENCOUNTERS AT KARISOKE

Fossey was only at Karisoke a short time when she encountered her first group of poachers. They wandered into her campsite, surprised to find a

Karisoke would be Fossey's home for many years. This is one of the permanent structures that Fossey later built there.

tall, light-skinned woman in their midst. They told her they knew of many gorillas in the area, and they even offered to bring her to a site where they'd seen some earlier that day. Fossey was angered by the mere fact that they were poachers, but she kept quiet about it and let them show her the gorilla site. Afterwards she thanked them, but she also told them that they had to stop poaching in her part of the forest. The poachers, who had lived in the forest all their lives, were surprised to receive such a stern warning from an outsider.

A few of the other white people who lived nearby and knew Fossey told her she had no right to give the poachers such a warning. They said the poachers poached because they needed the money and the food. In other words, they poached to survive. Fossey refused to see it that way. She could only see what they were doing to her beloved gorillas, selling their dried body parts as souvenirs and trapping babies to sell to zoos. When Fossey discovered an empty poacher's camp a

The Sun Didn't Shine Every Day

While there's little doubt that Fossey thought of her Karisoke campsite as a paradise, the environment could sometimes be very unfriendly. She wrote about mornings that were near-freezing—the opposite of many people's notion that the tropics are always warm—and pounding rainstorms falling from dark, ominous skies that could last for hours and sometimes whole days.

short time later, she destroyed all the weapons stored there and all the food they used as bait.

A few weeks after she set up the Karisoke camp, a visitor arrived—Alexie Forrester, the handsome young man whom Fossey had met while on her first African trip. Forrester had been in love with Fossey for years, and now, he decided, it was time for her to give up the gorilla project and get married. He showed up with an engagement ring, insisting that Fossey leave the camp to be with him.

Fossey was being forced to decide what she really wanted to do with her life. She chose to stay with the gorillas, and Forrester left with a broken heart. When Fossey told Leakey about the incident, he was thrilled. He told her the work was far too important to give up. Fossey would never see Forrester again.

Fossey went back to her work, and soon she was given the opportunity to see something many gorilla experts would never see in the wild—gorillas at play. She watched in utter fascination as the adults, powerful enough to break down small trees with one swing of their mighty arms, played gently with their young. She saw this not only as a breakthrough in gorilla observation but also as another sign of the gorillas' trust in her. They were clearly becoming more and more comfortable with this strange creature from the United States, who would sit nearby for hours with her camera and her notebook.

In June of the following year, Alan Root came to Karisoke with a film crew to begin work on a television documentary for *National Geographic* that would be shown around the world. Fossey was ready for them with thousands of photographs and pages of notes, plus the new cabin that had replaced the tent. It was already decorated with local art and looked very much like a permanent home. The crew stayed for two months and shot enough footage to make ten documentaries. Fossey was able to show them her camp as well as some of the gorillas she'd been studying. In time, the footage shot during this project would make her famous.

COCO AND PUCKER

A year or so went by with the usual routine—tracking the gorillas, getting used to life in the forest, shopping at the local villages, and occasionally traveling to visit friends and colleagues. Then, in February of 1969, Fossey had a troubling experience. When she returned to camp from a typical day of observation, she was told that a baby gorilla was being held captive in a nearby building and that it was very sick and needed immediate medical attention.

The building was owned by the Rwandan government, and the people who worked there were supposed to protect the animals in the area from poachers. When Fossey got there, she found a tiny gorilla so sick that it was near death. She stormed into the office of the man in charge and demanded to know how and why the animal was captured in the first place. The man explained that a poacher had been hired to capture the gorilla so it could be sent to a zoo in Germany. The man asked Fossey to nurse it back to health so it could make the trip.

Fossey was furious, but she held her temper so she could focus on what was most important—getting the animal back to her campsite and making sure it didn't die. For the next few weeks, she set aside all of her studies. She wasn't exactly sure what to do, as she didn't have any formal training in taking care of a sick gorilla. Knowing, however, that gorillas were biologically similar to humans, she followed common sense and hoped for the best.

There was a small storage area at the campsite where Fossey kept food, clothes, blankets, and other supplies. She moved all these items out and converted the room into a gorilla nursery. She covered the floor with fresh grass and branches, trying to copy the environment in which the gorilla would sleep if it were healthy and in the jungle. As with all of her other beloved gorillas, she gave this one a name—Coco. Once Coco's nursery was arranged, she went on a shopping spree, buying all the food she knew Coco would like—various fruits, vegetables, and canned milk—plus whatever medicines he required—vitamins, antibiotics, ointments, and so on.

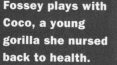

Fossey plays with Coco, a young gorilla she nursed back to health.

She cleaned Coco's nursery every day and fed him food and liquids mixed with medicine. Sometimes Coco fussed, probably because the medicine made everything taste awful. It certainly wasn't a taste he had ever encountered. Still, Fossey knew he had to have it, so she gently forced it on him. She wrote that he began to show signs of improvement after about a week.

A group of men arrived at Fossey's camp a few days later with a second sick gorilla—another one that had been captured by poachers and was heading to the zoo in Europe. Fossey was angrier than ever. She wrote a series of letters to anyone she thought would read them, asking them to find a way to keep the gorillas from going to the German zoo once they were healthy. While she waited for answers, she treated the second gorilla. It was a female, and she named her Pucker. Pucker was not as sick as Coco had been, but she was still in bad shape. Based on some unusual features of their bodies, Fossey felt certain Coco and Pucker were related.

Both gorillas were in good health after a few weeks, and Fossey began spending a little time in the forest again. Coco and Pucker would sometimes come with her. They would act normally when they were at the campsite, but beyond that, they would be shy and nervous. They had not forgotten the nightmare of being captured.

If anything good came out of the whole experience for Fossey, aside from the obvious pleasure of saving Coco and Pucker's lives, she was able to observe two gorillas more closely than she ever had before. She got to touch them, watch them eat and sleep, and listen to their sounds. She wrote pages and pages of notes and took hundreds of pictures. In the end, however, she could not save the pair from the fate that had been

Fossey enjoys taking a walk with Coco and Pucker. While she helped restore them to health, Fossey spent a lot of time studying their behavior.

planned for them—on May 3, 1969, they were put into crates, loaded onto a plane, and flown to Europe. Fossey was heartbroken.

A VISITOR WHO BECAME A FRIEND

Fossey packed Coco and Pucker in their crates with the help of a man named Robert Campbell. Campbell had arrived in Karisoke in April of 1969, assigned by *National Geographic* to shoot photos of Fossey and the gorillas for their magazine. Campbell was a quiet, gentle man who liked to keep things in his life in order and carefully organized.

Fossey set him up in his own cabin and hoped he would keep out of her way while she did her work. Unfortunately, that didn't happen—at the beginning of their relationship, Campbell followed Fossey like a shadow, taking hundreds of pictures. He didn't want to venture into the jungle alone, insisting that *National Geographic* wanted Fossey in as many of the pictures as possible. Because of this,

Fossey, who never liked visitors in the first place, couldn't stand Campbell.

Over time, however, her opinion of him changed. Fossey came to admire and care about the soft-spoken man in ways she had never cared

Robert Campbell took this photograph of Fossey during his stay at Karisoke.

about anyone before. Many people who visited Fossey during Campbell's stay at Karisoke say they were not aware of any strong personal feelings between them. They were certainly there, however.

A HISTORIC TOUCH

In early 1971, Fossey left Karisoke so she could earn her Ph.D. Louis Leakey had told her it was time for her to stop worrying about not being an officially trained scientist and go back to college to earn a doctoral degree. She wasn't too happy about leaving her jungle home and her beloved gorillas, but she knew it was necessary. "Without a Ph.D. at the least," she wrote, "it is very hard to get adequate grant support. . . ." Her work would always be questioned by the academic community until she became *Doctor* Dian Fossey.

Just before she left Karisoke, something amazing happened. She was in the forest observing Peanuts, a young male from a group of gorillas she called Group 8. Fossey felt she had a good relationship with Peanuts. Peanuts was up in a tree, watching her and playing. Then he came down

Africa in 1971

A lot was happening in Africa in 1971. In Uganda, Major General Idi Amin took power after leading a military coup to overthrow Prime Minister Milton Obote. Meanwhile, Congolese President Mobutu Sese Seko changed the name of his nation from the Democratic Republic of the Congo to Zaire.

from the tree to throw some leaves and beat his chest. He wasn't angry, but play-acting for Fossey. He came over to her and waited for her to do the same. Soon the two of them were doing impressions of each other.

Then Fossey decided to try and touch Peanuts. She held her hand out with her palm facing up. She thought this was best because the palm was the part of the human hand that looked most like a gorilla's hand, so it might look more familiar to Peanuts. At first, he was unsure what to do. Fossey didn't want to frighten him, so she set her hand down and waited. Finally, Peanuts took one more step, reached out, and touched Fossey's fingers. It was the first time a human being had ever made contact with a wild mountain gorilla. Best of all, Bob Campbell was there and captured the historic event on film. The pictures would later appear in an issue of *National Geographic*. It was one of the happiest moments of Fossey's life.

Weeks later, Fossey was in England, working toward her doctoral degree at

Fossey made physical contact with Peanuts, a gorilla in Group 8. This is one of Robert Campbell's photographs of their encounter.

Darwin College, which is part of Cambridge University. At first, she enjoyed being around young, energetic students and learning new things. Her enthusiasm didn't last, however. She was suddenly in the middle of a very structured world full of rules, deadlines, and expectations. After living in the wilds of Africa for so long, she wasn't sure that she could get used to this new life. She became depressed and wondered if earning a doctoral degree was all worth the trouble. Nevertheless, she did the best work she could.

Meanwhile, her dear friend Louis Leakey suffered a heart attack that confined him to bed for weeks. He was in his late sixties, but he was still leading the life of a man in his twenties. He worked all day, traveled constantly, and kept a full schedule. His aging body couldn't take the pressure. When he finally recovered, he went right back to this busy life. His friends and relatives told him he was making a mistake, but he didn't listen. He wasn't the type of person who could sit still. Fossey visited him while he was in the hospital, which cheered him up considerably.

EIGHT

The Famous *Doctor* Fossey

In January of 1970, the issue of *National Geographic* with Fossey on the cover and the amazing pictures Bob Campbell took of her touching Peanuts was released. Fossey received hundreds of letters from all over the world, from people who were suddenly enthralled with gorillas. Fossey also got letters from students who offered to come help her in Karisoke. She had provided them with inspiration, and they wanted to be just like her.

Louis Leakey decided to take advantage of Fossey's sudden fame. He held a dinner in Los Angeles, California, to raise money for his foundation. It cost $1,000 per person to attend the event. Obviously, only the wealthiest people could afford to go. Leakey featured Fossey as the guest speaker, and because of that, he filled the house and raised a great deal of money for his foundation. Fossey was understandably nervous. Because she spent so much of her time in the jungles of Africa, she wasn't used to being in front of huge crowds. She had no cause for worry, however. The crowd loved her. She turned the lights down and showed some of her best color slides on a giant screen while telling stories of her many adventures. When she was finished, the crowd's applause was almost deafening.

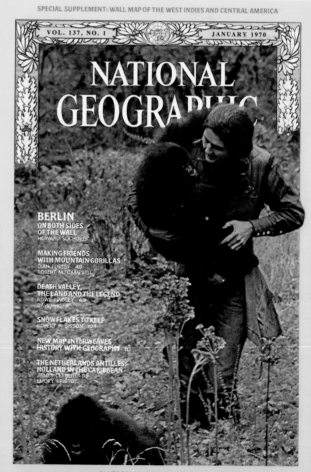

Fossey and her work became internationally known after she was featured in *National Geographic*.

By March of 1971, Fossey was finished with the first part of her doctoral courses and returned to Karisoke. She was a very different person. She was more educated, more famous, and had more money. She had visited the people who were paying for her work at Karisoke and asked for more. They were more than happy to give it to her. With the extra money, she could expand her research area. It was time for Karisoke to grow.

FRESH NEW FACES

Fossey received offers from students to come and help, and she decided to accept some of them. These young people would essentially be her employees. Fossey chose only the most serious-minded young men and women who could help her do all the work she couldn't handle. There just wasn't enough time in the day for her to do everything she wanted to do, so these eager students were very welcome.

The Leakey Foundation

Louis Leakey founded the Leakey Foundation in 1968 for the purpose of studying human origins and evolution. It gives sums of money called grants to people or groups devoted to furthering this study. Grants can be given to people for traveling around the world to conduct research, or to those who wish to further their education by studying human origins. Each year it gives more than $600,000 to field researchers alone.

With the help of her growing student staff and her old friends from Rwanda, she went about building more tents and cabins. Some were set close to her own cabin, while others were built deeper in the forest in places that were too far away for Fossey to reach on foot every day but still had gorilla groups that needed to be studied. Karisoke was becoming something of a small town.

Early 1972 saw another major change to the Karisoke family—Bob Campbell, the photographer sent by *National Geographic* to capture some of the most amazing images of mountain gorillas ever seen, left in March to return home after almost three years. By this time, Fossey had developed a deep attachment to him and was heartbroken to see him go. She stayed in her cabin until he was gone, and many who knew Fossey say she never fully got over the loss.

There were problems to tackle, however, so Fossey couldn't dwell on her personal troubles. Poaching was a big problem—she was certain that it always would be—but she was figuring out new ways of dealing with it. Most of the poachers believed in black magic, which included the casting of spells and the calling of spirits. These beliefs were part of their larger belief in the Vodou religion (often misspelled "voodoo"), which puts people in touch with the spirit world that is home to greater godlike beings and the spirits of the deceased. These other-worldly beings, the African natives thought, had ultimate power over the lives of the living. Fossey figured out ways to use this against the poachers. She would put on Halloween masks and throw gasoline into her campfire at night to put on a frightening show. Sometimes she would tell poachers that she would put a curse on them or make certain spirits angry with them if they didn't leave the gorillas alone.

While this usually didn't discourage them entirely, it often kept the poachers away for a little while.

By 1972, Fossey had counted nearly one hundred gorillas in her study area that made up almost ten different groups. As usual, Fossey made a point of giving each gorilla a name. One was called Whinny because of the strange, horselike sounds he made. There was also Uncle Bert, named after one of Fossey's favorite uncles. Another was Amok. Amok was the half-brother of Uncle Bert. There was also one she named Digit.

THE GREATEST OF THEM ALL

Digit was a large male who got his name because one of his fingers had been broken at some point, and when it healed, it looked a bit crooked and twisted (*digit* is another word for a finger or a toe). Fossey first encountered him in 1967, and by 1972, they were close friends. More than any other gorilla Fossey had studied, Digit seemed to like Fossey and enjoy having her around. He would approach her without fear, and they would touch each other's hands and face. What an amazing scientific breakthrough this was! When Fossey began her studies at Karisoke, no one had ever touched a wild mountain gorilla. Now Fossey and Digit were exchanging embraces like dear friends.

Digit was a part of a group Fossey called Group 4. Because Digit welcomed Fossey, soon the rest of the group did too. Eventually, she was even allowed to touch the babies—something many scientists thought was impossible. Fossey would play with them as if they were her own children. Pretty soon Digit was even welcoming Fossey's friends. Fossey

Fossey developed a special affection for Digit, a member of Group 4. She took this photograph of him.

would write in her famous book, *Gorillas in the Mist*, that Digit would ignore her completely in order to check out anyone new she brought along.

Most gorilla groups consist of a variety of gorillas of different ages and genders. The leader of a group is almost always a large silverback male. They are called silverbacks because the dark hair on their backs begins turning gray with age. Thus, the silverback leaders are always older and fully matured. There are also a few younger males, one of whom might take over as the leader when the silverback dies. There are also some older females, and then there are the babies. All of the adults—both male and female—gather the food, build the nests, and protect the young. The average gorilla group has a total of between five and fifteen members.

Digit was not a silverback when Fossey first encountered him in 1967, and in 1972 he was still one of the secondary males. Still, he was definitely becoming stronger, older, and wiser. Many of the males who reached this age either went off and formed their own groups or tried to take over the leadership role of their present group. Fossey was happy to see that, as Digit grew, he did not leave Group 4, nor did he lose his love for her. One rainy day, while observing his group from a distance, she suddenly found his giant, hairy arm on her shoulder and looked up to find him standing beside her. He then sat down, wanting to be close to his friend. During this incredible encounter, Fossey decided to lay her head in his lap.

OTHER WILD FRIENDS

Fossey's gift for interacting with animals was not confined to just gorillas. She had many other animal friends at Karisoke. She had a rooster she named Desi, after Desi Arnaz of the legendary TV show *I Love Lucy*. She also had a pair of black ravens named Charles and Yvonne who would fly into camp whenever they got hungry. She had a dog named Cindy, who was given to her by some friends who lived nearby. She had always

In addition to her work with mountain gorillas, Fossey kept several pets, including a dog named Cindy.

wanted a dog as a child but never had one, so she felt strongly about Cindy.

Then there was Kima, a blue monkey. Fossey's friends, some of whom had kept monkeys as pets before, warned her that Kima would cause a lot of trouble. Fossey decided to ignore their advice. In no time at all, Kima was making a mess of Fossey's cabin, emptying drawers onto the floor and throwing her notes around. She even bit Fossey a few times and would often attack visitors. Fossey eventually accepted this as normal monkey behavior.

While she certainly loved having all these animal friends, Fossey also had some scary experiences because of them. Once, her dog Cindy was kidnapped by a poacher named Munyarukiko. He was one of the more experienced poachers and was one of Fossey's greatest enemies. Munyarukiko most likely kidnapped Cindy in an attempt to get even with Fossey for destroying so many of his traps and weapons.

When Fossey heard about this, she was furious. Munyarukiko, she knew, was also the man responsible for taking Coco and Pucker from the forest and selling them to the European zoo years earlier. When she found out where Cindy was being held, she sent some of her staff to the poachers' camp wearing Halloween masks and carrying firecrackers. As night fell, they scared the wits out of the poachers and brought Cindy back safely.

In March of 1973, a poacher named Seregera, who had gone to prison some years earlier for his poaching activities, was set free. He entered Fossey's study area, setting traps and putting together new poaching groups. When Fossey found out about this, she and her staff members went about patrolling the area, destroying the traps and whatever weapons they could find.

Seregera answered this by setting even more traps. He and his men embarked on an ambitious trap-setting crusade that lasted for days. There were literally hundreds of traps now, and the gorilla group that was most vulnerable to them was Group 5. Fossey and her staff tried to destroy as many of the traps as they could, but she knew they wouldn't get all of them, so she decided to try to herd Group 5 away from the trap-infested area instead. This made the gorillas extremely upset, and Fossey was infuriated that she had been forced to do it.

MORE NEW FACES

More students came and went as the years passed, and Karisoke continued to grow. One of those students was Kelly Stewart, daughter of famed actor Jimmy Stewart. In spite of the fact that she came from a wealthy family, she was very down-to-earth and, as Fossey would note with admiration, very intelligent. She was truly interested in the study of gorillas and would endure the bad weather, animal attacks, and filthy cabins the same way everyone else did.

Like Fossey, Stewart kept notes on all her findings and observations, and as time passed, these notes piled up. Then, one night in early November of 1975, while Fossey and Kelly were talking outside Fossey's cabin, one of Fossey's Rwandan helpers came running into the campsite, screaming. The cabin in which Stewart was staying was on fire! Later Fossey would determine that Stewart had hung some clothing too close to the stove so it would dry, and it had ignited. It took them half the night to put the fire out. The loss of the cabin was bad, but the loss of most of Stewart's notes was devastating.

In May of 1976, Fossey received some good news. She went back to England to perform the final stages of her Ph.D. studies and, at last, graduated with a degree in zoology. She was officially Doctor Dian Fossey. Sadly, her dear friend Louis Leakey, the man who had given her nearly everything and had always supported her, was not alive to enjoy this achievement with her. He'd had a second heart attack in 1972 that ended his life.

Fossey visited California next. She took part in a series of lectures that also included the two other women Leakey had helped in the scientific world—Jane Goodall, whom Fossey had already befriended, and a Canadian named Biruté Galdikas, who was studying orangutans on the island of Borneo. To see all three members of Leakey's famous team in the same place was truly a treat for the audience. The three women posed for pictures and signed autographs.

Fossey returned to Karisoke that summer, excited to get back to work. More students were coming and going, and Fossey did her best to manage them. She didn't get along with some of them, but others became true friends. One was a young man named Tim White. White wasn't really a student, but more of a drifter. Along with his backpack and the few supplies he needed to survive, he traveled around the world, visiting places he thought might be interesting. While Fossey didn't usually waste time with people like this, she took a liking to White. He helped with her gorilla studies in whatever way she asked, and he was good at fixing things. He kept all the lights and stoves running efficiently.

White left Karisoke in December of 1976. Fossey was sad to see him go, but she was happy about his replacement, a young man from

Biruté Galdikas

Biruté Galdikas was born in Germany in 1948. Her family moved to Canada a year later. She went to college both in Canada and the United States, earning degrees in biology, psychology, and anthropology. She went to Borneo to study orangutans in 1971. At that time, less was known about orangutans than any of the other apes. Through decades of careful observation, Galdikas learned that orangutans usually live alone and eat mostly fruits, but will also consume leaves, flowers, tree bark, and sometimes insects. In 1986, she created a foundation for orangutan conservation, and in 1995, she published a book called *Reflections of Eden: My Years with the Orangutans of Borneo.*

Ian Redmond and a Rwandan student assistant pet Fossey's dog Cindy. Redmond would be an important part of Fossey's team.

England named Ian Redmond. Redmond was not as organized as Fossey was, and there were days when she wondered if he'd be able to make it in the wilds of Africa. "Ian . . . arrives at 7:30 or so," she wrote, "wearing no shorts and no shoes—crazy. For sure this kid is not going to work out." However, he had great determination and, much to Fossey's delight, the same love and devotion to the protection of animals. In the years ahead, he would prove to be a great help to Fossey in her fight against poachers.

By the end of the year, Fossey was working almost around the clock. She would take notes and pictures while tracking the gorilla groups during the day and then sit at her typewriter at night. Now that she was *Dr.* Fossey, more was expected of her than ever before. People wanted her to write articles and papers to share with the academic community. She had also promised to write a book that could be sold in ordinary bookstores. This book would become *Gorillas in the Mist*, which would turn into an international best-seller. Sadly, though, the giant workload was taking its toll on her health. She was stubborn too. She didn't want to stop working, so she ignored her health problems and hoped for the best.

NINE

Dark Days Ahead

By the summer of 1977, Fossey's health problems were getting worse, and she was beginning to grow concerned. In August, she went to a hospital in the Rwandan town of Ruhengeri. One of the doctors was a friend of hers. After a careful checkup and a series of X-rays, the doctor feared she might be developing a very serious case of tuberculosis, which affects one's breathing. The fact that she was a longtime smoker didn't help, either.

The doctor told her she had to be treated immediately. She went to see a team of specialists in the United States. She received a mixture of good and bad news from the U.S. doctors. The good news was they did not find any evidence of tuberculosis. The bad news was she still needed an operation. She had broken a rib some months earlier, and although the rib healed on its own, splinters from the broken bone had scattered. They performed surgery and removed the splinters.

By December of 1977, Fossey was back at Karisoke and in a generally happy mood. The poachers had been quiet in recent months, and she and her staff had their yearly Christmas party. All in all, she believed, things were looking pretty good.

THE DAY EVERYTHING CHANGED

During the first week of 1978, Fossey had been wanting to study Group 4—the group that contained, among others, Uncle Bert and her beloved Digit, but she was having trouble locating it. So she sent Ian Redmond and one of the African trackers out to find the group. A few miles from the campsite the two men saw signs of a massive struggle between gorillas

Tuberculosis in Africa

Tuberculosis was one of the most common and widespread diseases in Africa when Fossey was there. It was probably introduced to the country by European settlers in the 1600s or 1700s. During the early 1900s, as Africa became more industrialized and people started living in crowded cities, the disease spread. By the mid-1950s, it had grown to epidemic proportions. Tuberculosis is a bacterial infection that usually infects the lungs. Symptoms include coughing, chest pain, fever, weight loss, and shortness of breath, and, if left untreated, death.

and humans. About a hundred yards further on, Redmond came upon Digit's body. He'd been murdered by a band of poachers.

Redmond ran back to the campsite. When he got there, he was barely able to get the words out. Fossey would later write that the news of Digit's death changed her forever. She was paralyzed by shock and rage. Nevertheless, even through the pain, she promised herself that her dear friend would not have died for nothing. She would see that, somehow, something good came of it.

Fossey began writing letters to people she believed would help her protect the gorillas. One of the people who received a letter was the president of Rwanda, Juvénal Habyarimana. Habyarimana was familiar with Fossey's work and knew that posters had been sent all around the world with Digit's picture on them, encouraging people to come to Rwanda to see the famous gorillas. That brought a lot of money into Rwanda, which the country needed very badly. Fossey asked the president to make sure the people who killed Digit, once they were captured, were given the harshest punishment allowed by Rwandan law.

She also wrote to *National Geographic*. She said that she was particularly enraged by the fact that the poachers had attacked gorillas in one of her work groups, and if they were allowed to get away with that, it wouldn't be long before they went after *all* the groups. She said her plan was to let as many magazines and newspapers as possible know about the poachers. She wanted everyone in the world to know what the poachers were doing.

Another idea came from Ian Redmond. Fossey didn't like it at first, but eventually she decided it couldn't be avoided—try to raise money in order to put together a team of people whose only job would be to patrol the area to keep poaching under control. Fossey didn't like this at first because she didn't want to be seen as a military commander building up a private army. She was a zoologist, after all, sent into Africa by Louis Leakey to study gorillas. She wasn't supposed to be involved in jungle warfare. Although Rwanda already had a team of trained guards in the area who were supposed to be controlling the poaching problem, Fossey knew she couldn't depend on them. After all, they had held Coco captive before he was shipped off to the German zoo.

THE DIGIT FUND

Reluctantly, Fossey agreed to give Ian Redmond's idea a try. She started something called the Digit Fund, which she hoped would provide the

Ian Redmond holds one of the many poachers' snares found in the woods. Redmond suggested that regular patrols of the area might help keep poachers away.

money she needed to launch her own antipoaching patrol. In the meantime, Fossey buried Digit's body in a grave just outside her cabin. She made a little marker for him and lovingly wrote his name in simple, black letters.

Fossey certainly had her suspicions about who had killed Digit, and she didn't have to wait long to find out for sure. The very next day, a young poacher had the nerve to venture near the campsite. In the past, poachers never went too close to camp because they were terrified of Fossey. One of Fossey's helpers spotted the poacher, and soon he was captured and brought back to face her. He wore a shirt still stained with Digit's blood, and Fossey would later write that she was barely able to keep herself from locking her hands around his neck. After asking many questions, she learned the names of all the poachers who had killed Digit. Sure enough, at the top of the list, was Munyarukiko.

Fossey was deeply saddened by Digit's death and wanted to do more to stop the gorilla poachers.

Fossey kept writing letters, trying to let people know that they could help stop the slaughter of gorillas by giving money to the Digit Fund. Money began coming in from various places. Questions about whether or not the money should be put toward the creation of the "army," about who had the right to most of the money, and about whether it was even legal to bring money into Rwanda for these reasons quickly followed. Many of the people who were making the decisions about the Digit Fund had different opinions about where the money should go. Some of the people had never been to Africa, had never seen a mountain gorilla, and had no idea what horrors the gorillas were being forced to endure at the hands of the ruthless poachers. Fossey, who knew these horrors almost as well as the gorillas themselves did, was thousands of miles away and was not being consulted.

The situation quickly turned into a huge mess, which only made Fossey angrier. While thousands and thousands of dollars had been given to the Digit Fund, very little of it actually ended up in Fossey's pocket. So, as ridiculous as it may sound, the money wasn't being used for what the Digit Fund had been created for in the first place. Meanwhile, the poaching continued. Munyarukiko, who still hadn't been punished for Digit's death, became bolder than ever. He was sure nothing would happen to him now.

Life at Karisoke went from bad to worse. In May of 1978, Ian Redmond left the camp to go back home to England. He'd stayed as long as he could, helping Fossey form her antipoaching forces. He was a faithful worker right until the end, destroying dozens of traps during his last sweep through the jungle. He promised Fossey he would return, but he had things to do back home. After he left, she felt more alone than ever. Redmond was not only a friend but an ally, someone who understood her fight and accepted it as his own.

With Redmond gone and almost no money coming in from the Digit Fund, the poachers kept going. In July, they shot and killed Uncle Bert, the leader of Group 4, along with some others. When Fossey found out why, she was beside herself. Someone had offered money for one of the group's babies. In order to get it, the poachers knew they'd have to kill the adults. Fossey later determined that Uncle Bert had fought off the poachers as long as he could while the others escaped. The poachers never got the baby, whom Fossey had named Kweli, so Uncle Bert had done his job right down to his last breath.

The Struggle for the Digit Fund

In England, the Digit Fund—called the "Mountain Gorilla Fund UK" in that country—was run by the Faunal Preservation Society (FPS). At first, Fossey was pleased about this. Then she learned that the FPS planned to send the money to the Rwandan government agents who were supposedly managing the park that contained the gorillas. Fossey knew they would keep this money for themselves rather than give it to her. They would buy new cars and build huts for the guards, not patrol the forest.

The gorilla named Uncle Bert was killed by poachers while trying to protect other members of his group.

Fossey wrote in her journals that she was certain she could have saved Uncle Bert and the others if she'd had the money that was supposed to come from the Digit Fund. "If they had only sent *me* the money people in England gave for the Digit Fund, I would have hired enough patrols to drive the poachers off the mountain months ago!"

TEN

Professor Fossey

By 1978, Fossey was concerning herself less with actual gorilla studies and more with the war against the poachers. Without Louis Leakey to keep her on the right track, she was changing into something other than a zoologist. In spite of the fact that she had earned a doctoral degree, many people in the academic community never really thought of her as a true scientist. For one thing, she hadn't gone to school for zoology in the years before she earned her Ph.D. When she had gone to college in California, her courses had nothing to do with gorillas. Many felt she had reached her position only because of Leakey's kindness. Now that she was losing sight of her studies, those same people were wondering if maybe Leakey really had made a mistake in choosing her for the project. Fossey was supposed to be watching the gorillas, after all, not waging a war.

BEING NUDGED OUT

Because of this, many people began wondering if the Karisoke research area would be better off if Fossey were no longer in control of it. There was, for example, a conservation organization called the World Wildlife Fund that had given a few thousand dollars to Fossey's Digit Fund, but many of the people who ran it worried that their organization would look bad if they continued giving money to a woman who was developing such a bad reputation. The U.S. government was also concerned that one of its citizens was breaking Rwandan laws by attacking poachers and destroying their property out of revenge. She was also hostile toward tourists, once firing her pistol into the air to scare off a group of them. The Rwandan government certainly wouldn't put up with Fossey's bad behavior forever. Even the people at *National Geographic* were wondering if they should stop giving Fossey money.

Fossey found all of this hard to swallow. She had established Karisoke and built it up on her own. She couldn't understand how anyone could demand that she leave it behind. She had been isolated in the middle of the jungle for too long to fully understand the negative reputation she was developing. It was one thing to want to save gorillas' lives, but it was another to actively and aggressively attack the people who were hurting them. By doing so, Fossey was giving conservation efforts a bad name.

In August of 1979, a man named Glenn Hausfater came to Karisoke. He was a professor at Cornell University in Ithaca, New York. Hausfater was visiting Karisoke to further his own study of gorillas. He was a cheerful, intelligent man, and he and Fossey got along well. It wasn't long before she told him the story of how some people wanted her to leave Karisoke. She mentioned that she didn't so much mind the idea of going back to the United States for a while, but there was nothing for her to do there.

Hausfater had an idea—Fossey should become a teacher at Cornell. She would be a visiting professor, which meant she would only be there for a short time rather than as a permanent part of its staff. The university was also, Hausfater pointed out, interested in having more women professors. Fossey loved the idea and accepted a teaching position for a term that would begin that March. While she prepared to leave Karisoke to begin her new life in Ithaca, she received some news that her old enemy, the master poacher Munyarukiko, had died a mysterious death.

Fossey wondered if she'd be able to fit in at Cornell because she had been away from "civilized" life for so long. As it turned out, she had no trouble at all. She enjoyed being around bright and energetic young people. Cornell wasn't just a school, it was its own little world, as separate from the larger world as Karisoke was. Fossey's students were thrilled to have such a famous person teaching them, and she discovered that she liked being a teacher. She also rented a small apartment and a car, and she was earning a salary. In many ways this period in her life served to help her "recharge her emotional batteries." She knew that someday she would return to Africa to continue studying and protecting her beloved gorillas.

Meanwhile, Karisoke was being run by a man named Sandy Harcourt. Harcourt was a student when he first met Fossey in the 1970s. He was smart and ambitious and eventually would earn a doctoral

Fossey says good-bye to Karisoke to return the United States.

degree of his own. Fossey liked him at first, but over time she came to distrust him. When others were pushing to have her removed from Karisoke, Harcourt was trying to get those same people to believe he was the perfect person to take her place. He eventually got the job and decided to turn Karisoke back into a research center only. He wanted the people at Karisoke to focus on gathering research data about gorillas and not to worry so much about poachers. This didn't make Fossey happy, but at the time, there was very little she could do about it.

A NOT-SO-BRILLIANT IDEA AFTER ALL

Harcourt ended up leaving Karisoke after a few years. This was partially because he was having trouble living the kind of isolated jungle life that Fossey had grown used to. It was also because the people who wanted him to take the job in the first place began to lose faith in him. He could be a difficult person to deal with. He sometimes made ridiculous demands and wrote nasty letters. Also, Karisoke did not seem to improve much under his leadership. Fossey was not surprised. She believed she was the only person who truly knew how to run the place. So, only a few years after Fossey had been forced out of Karisoke, the people who'd forced her out admitted that they'd made a mistake.

Fossey was still teaching at Cornell at the beginning of 1983, but the things she was hearing about Karisoke from the students and friends who'd been there disturbed her. Poaching was as bad as it had ever been. The cabins were falling apart. People were losing interest, both in visiting and in giving money to the research center. Clearly, it was time for

At Cornell, Fossey discovered she liked being a teacher and being a part of the educational community. When she heard that there were problems at Karisoke, however, she made plans to go back.

Fossey to return. First, however, she wanted to finish up the commitments she'd made to the students at Cornell. She also wanted to finish writing the book that would eventually become a worldwide best-seller and a Hollywood movie, *Gorillas in the Mist*.

Cold War Heats Up

The "Cold War" was a conflict between the two superpowers of the world, the United States and the Union of Soviet Socialist Republic (USSR), in the 1900s. Tensions between the two countries began at the end of World War II, when they disagreed on who would then control war-torn Europe. The leaders of the USSR followed *communist* beliefs (large government control over the people), whereas the U.S. leaders followed *capitalist* beliefs (small government, people make more of their own choices). The United States obviously wanted as many other capitalist countries as possible, whereas the USSR wanted them to be communist. Both sides began to increase the number of nuclear and other types of weapons in effort to show each other how powerful they were. By the early 1980s, President Ronald Reagan called the USSR an "Evil Empire" and worked on developing a system for intercepting incoming missiles in the event that the Soviets attacked the United States.

Fossey returned to Karisoke and plunged into her work.

ELEVEN

Back to Karisoke for Good

Fossey arrived in Africa in June of 1983 and soon returned to the place she loved more than any other. Her faithful staff members were waiting for her, and she hugged and greeted every one of them. Then she turned her attention to the camp itself, and what she saw made her cry. Karisoke had truly been left to ruin. Most of her things were either broken or gone. Lights and stoves didn't work. The floors and walls were filthy beyond description. Even the gorilla graveyard, which she thought of as a holy place, had been consumed by vines, shrubs, and other vegetation. With the help of the others, Fossey worked day and night to return everything to its former glory. Within a week, Karisoke looked like its old self again.

Once she had the camp in order, it was time to visit the gorillas. Again, Fossey became worried. She wondered how many were left and if they were healthy. She also worried that they might not remember her. It had been so many years. She wasn't sure if she could handle the rejection if they treated her like a stranger after all the time she'd spent with them.

She managed to find one of the old females from Group 5 whom she had named Effie. Effie had had a baby in her absence whom Fossey named Maggie. When Effie first spotted Fossey, she gave her a quick look and that was it. Then, apparently in shock, she looked again, and Fossey realized Effie recognized her. After that, another female whom Fossey had named Tuck appeared and ran over to her. Fossey lay down on the jungle floor, and Tuck lay beside her, then embraced her. She would later write that, after being away from Karisoke for so long, she was sure she would never leave again. This was truly her home and would be forever.

Once Fossey had settled back into life at Karisoke, she began her antipoaching efforts again. In one month alone, she and her patrols found and destroyed more than four hundred traps. They also captured a veteran poacher named Sebahutu and had him put in jail for a five-year sentence. By the end of the year, more poachers were caught and thrown in jail, and more than 1,500 traps were destroyed.

Sadly, Fossey was running low on money. Fewer people were giving grants to pay for Karisoke's upkeep, and Fossey was often paying her staff out of her own pocket. She'd earned some money while teaching at Cornell, some from writing *Gorillas in the Mist*, and some from all the lectures she gave. Still, even that wouldn't last forever. Most of the money

Fossey and her staff found and destroyed hundreds of traps.

donated to the Digit Fund was still ending up everywhere except where it was needed most—in Fossey's pocket, so she could pay people to patrol the area for poachers.

FOSSEY'S NEWEST ENEMY

At the same time, ironically, the Rwandan government was making more money off the gorillas than ever before. With the release of Fossey's book and all the news coverage she had received, more and more people were coming to Rwanda to see the famous gorillas of the Virunga Mountains. This would be the start of something called "ecotourism."

Ecotourism is the practice of visiting interesting places for the purpose of studying their environments, learning about the efforts being undertaken to preserve those environments, and benefiting the people and the wildlife that are native to them. Ideal locations for ecotourism usually are wild environments that are in danger of disappearing due to humankind's ever-growing need to build and develop, such as the rain forests of Central and South America. The more houses, gas stations, and shopping malls humans build, the fewer places there are for plants and animals to thrive.

Because more and more ecotourists were coming to Rwanda, Rwanda was making money that the country needed very badly. However, Fossey was not pleased about the sudden wave of tourists. Many of the people who showed up at her doorstep were little more than wealthy people looking for a quick thrill. They would demand that Fossey take them into the jungle and show them the gorillas as if she were a tour guide. They didn't realize that Karisoke was a real scientific research center. They were often rude and arrogant, throwing garbage on the ground as if they were at an amusement park.

More often than not, Fossey would be rude right back to them, often throwing them out of Karisoke and telling them to go back home. This upset not only the visitors, it also upset the Rwandan government. The government officials didn't want people around the world hearing about this or else the ecotourists would stop coming.

Rwandan leaders pleaded with Fossey to behave herself, but she refused. She knew that the money coming in from the ecotourists would be beneficial to the gorillas in some ways. For example, because the gorillas were the reason most of the tourists were coming, the Rwandan government likely would make more of an effort to help protect them. Fossey certainly didn't have a problem with that. As a scientist, however, and the one who knew the gorillas better than anyone, she also saw a danger that everyone else was ignoring. The gorillas weren't used to being around so

All of the visitors to Rwanda were creating problems for the mountain gorillas.

many humans, so it was just matter of time before they became infected with a human disease that their bodies couldn't handle. This nightmare became a reality when one of the gorillas—whom Fossey named Nunkie—that had become trained to interact with tourists and was supposedly in good health, suddenly died.

Another problem arose. Many of the gorillas in her study groups were beginning to act strangely. They were breaking away from their groups and wandering. They were showing less interest in protecting their young. They weren't eating. Fossey was having trouble finding them in the usual places. She couldn't understand why all this was happening, but was certain that it had a lot to do with the sudden onrush of visitors from all over the world.

Clearly, she thought, something terrible was beginning to happen. First and foremost, she wanted to know what had killed Nunkie. In October of 1985, she contacted a number of doctors and veterinarians whom she could trust—those who were not associated with ecotourism and therefore would give their honest opinions about what had happened. The results terrified her. Nunkie's intestines were loaded with parasites. They weren't parasites found in gorillas, either. They were parasites normally found in humans.

Fossey knew this information was extremely sensitive. If word got out that the presence of humans was truly harmful to the gorillas, the tourists would stop coming, and the money would stop coming too. Fossey hoped no one would find out about Nunkie's parasites. Then, on October 27, she received a horrible warning. Unable to sleep, she opened her door and found a wooden carving of a viper on the ground before her. It was, she knew, the sign that someone had put a death curse on her.

Fossey noticed a dramatic change in the behavior of the mountain gorillas because of all of the tourists. She could no longer find the groups in their usual habitats.

Fossey tried to carry on with her life at Karisoke as best she could, putting the curse out of her mind. She caught another longtime poacher and had him put in jail for a three-year term. She also learned that another nasty poacher whom she had put in jail years earlier had gotten into a fight and had died as a result. She also received the good news that, in spite of the many enemies she'd made in Rwanda, she'd been given permission to stay in the country for another two years.

THE DEATH OF DIAN FOSSEY

Sadly, Fossey would not live through those two years. During the evening of December 26, she sat down to write a letter to a friend. Before she finished it, she wrote the following in her journal:

When you realize the value of all life, you dwell less on what is past and concentrate more on the preservation of the future.

The next morning, just as the sun was lighting Karisoke's misty meadow, one of Fossey's former helpers, a Rwandan named Kanyaragana, came into her cabin and found her dead. She'd been murdered. Furniture was overturned and clothes and other items were scattered everywhere. Clearly, there had been a struggle. Fossey also had a gun at her side, one that she kept for protection, but it hadn't been fired. She never had the chance. Further investigation of the crime scene revealed that a corner of the corrugated metal "skin" of her cabin had been peeled back, suggesting the killer's mode of entry.

The mystery of who killed Fossey has never been answered. The courts in Rwanda, eager to squash any fear that their country was a dangerous place and thus losing millions of dollars from ecotourism, convicted two men of the murder. One was a tracker named Rwelekana who worked on Fossey's staff. The other was Wayne McGuire, a student from Oklahoma University who was also on Fossey's staff and, notably, the only American at Karisoke apart from Fossey herself. Interestingly, after being taken to prison, Rwelekana supposedly committed suicide in his cell. Most believe, however, that he had nothing to do with Fossey's murder, but possibly knew who did and was murdered so he wouldn't talk. As for McGuire, the Rwandan court, in a trial that took less than an hour, convicted McGuire on the basis that he wanted to steal Fossey's research notes. Those who knew McGuire, however, said that the charge was ridiculous and knew he could never commit such a horrible act, regardless of the motive. Before McGuire could be arrested by Rwandan authorities, he fled the country and headed back to the United States. Interestingly, the Rwandan authorities have never tried to get McGuire back into their country, perhaps further proof that they know he really didn't murder Fossey.

So who did? The FBI, which has kept the case open all these years focused on a man named Protais Zigiranyirazo. At the time of Fossey's death, Zigiranyirazo was the son-in-law of then-Rwandan president Juvénal Habyarimana. He was also the mastermind behind poaching and smuggling efforts throughout the country. Fossey apparently knew this and supposedly was getting ready to expose him to the rest of the world when she died. Her hope was for someone to put a stop to his illegal activities. This worried him, as he would lose thousands, possibly even millions, of dollars. His relation to the Rwandan president, however, put him "above the law." Then, in 1994, President Habyarimana was assassinated, and Zigiranyirazo didn't have that protection anymore. He escaped

Rwanda but was captured in Belgium in 2001. The people running the Rwandan government at the time were all but certain that Zigiranyirazo was responsible for Fossey's death. He probably didn't commit the actual killing, but they believe he was the person who gave the order for it to be done. Hopefully, the matter will eventually be resolved.

Four days after the killing, on December 31, Fossey's body was buried in the gorilla graveyard by her cabin, alongside her beloved Digit. Her funeral was attended by her staff and her closest friends. Sadly, the person who killed her was never found. Some say it was a poacher seeking revenge. Others believe it was someone hired by the people who wanted to make even more money through ecotourism and had to get Fossey out of the way. Perhaps in time, all the answers will come to light, but for now they remain a mystery.

Dian Fossey devoted her life to the protection and study of the gorillas of the Virunga Mountains. Through her efforts, more is now known about these remarkable animals' habits and behavior than ever

Gorillas in the Mist, the Movie

The movie version of Dian Fossey's life, which was based largely on her book of the same name, was released in 1988. Sigourney Weaver, who would eventually win a Golden Globe Award for her performance, played the role of Dian Fossey. The movie was tremendously popular and made the public more aware of Fossey's work. Much of the film was shot in Kenya.

before. She erased the popular belief that mountain gorillas were ruthless, brutal creatures, bent on killing and destruction. Instead, Fossey showed the world that they were gentle, intelligent, and caring, especially when it came to nurturing their young. She harbored a passion that was infectious. Her love for the mountain gorillas spread across the globe. As a result, more efforts have been made to protect gorillas and to continue studying them in the hopes that they might shed more light on human evolution.

Although Fossey died during her great mission, Karisoke remains open to this day and is used by students from all over the world. Her memory serves as a stark reminder of how important it is to stand by our principles and fight for what we believe is right. Fossey continues to be an inspiration to those who care about the natural resources of the world. Her good work lives through the lives of those she touched, and those who want to make certain that her decades of devotion will not go to waste.

Staff members and friends said good-bye to a great animal activist and zoologist during Fossey's funeral service on December 31, 1985.

Fossey's work with mountain gorillas continues on through the efforts of the Dian Fossey Gorilla Fund International and the staff at Karisoke.

Timeline

1952 Dr. Jonas Salk discovers a vaccine for polio.

1954 Fossey graduates from San Jose State College with a degree in occupational therapy.

1955 Fossey moves to Louisville, Kentucky, and takes an administrative position at the Kosair Crippled Children's Hospital.

1959 Hawaii and Alaska become U.S. states. Fidel Castro takes power in Cuba after a military coup removes President Fulgencio Batista from power.

1962 The African nation of Uganda gains its independence and elects its first leader, Milton Obote. In the fall, the world holds its breath while the United States and the Soviet Union reach the brink of nuclear war during what would become known as the Cuban Missile Crisis.

1963 After taking out a loan to finance the trip, Fossey travels to Africa in September. While in the African nation of Kenya, she meets famed paleontologist Louis Leakey. She tells Leakey she is interested in studying mountain gorillas.

1963 On November 22, American president John F. Kennedy is assassinated in Dallas, Texas.

1966 Louis Leakey comes to Louisville to give a lecture, and Fossey attends. He remembers her and asks if she'd be interested in traveling to the Virunga Mountains in the African Congo to study the mountain gorillas full-time. Fossey accepts and leaves Louisville in December.

1967 In July, fighting breaks out in the Congo between the existing government and rebel forces. Fossey is forced to leave her mountain encampment for her own safety. In September, she sets up a second camp, which she calls Karisoke, in Rwanda, between the Karisimbi and Visoke mountains.

1968 In June, shortly after winning a major primary election for president, Robert Kennedy, brother of assassinated president John F. Kennedy, is himself assassinated in a hotel kitchen.

1970 In January, Fossey makes history by making physical contact with one of the gorillas. The moment is captured on film by photographer Robert Campbell.

1972 Louis Leakey dies in October after suffering his second heart attack.

1975 The African nation of Mozambique is granted its independence by the European nation of Portugal.

1976 Fossey earns her Ph.D. in zoology.

1977 In Africa, the Shab province of Zaire is attacked by troops from Angola. Fifteen hundred soldiers from Morocco are immediately transferred to the area, and the attackers are defeated.

1978 One of Fossey's favorite gorillas, whom she named Digit, is found dead, the victim of poachers. Fossey founds the Digit Fund, a global fund-raising organization, so she can hire people to destroy poachers' traps and patrol the mountains.

1979 Fossey is offered a teaching position at Cornell University in New York, and accepts.

1979 Idi Amin, leader of Uganda and one of the most brutal rulers in Africa's history, is overthrown by Tazanian troops and Ugandan rebels.

1983 After roughly four years as a professor at Cornell, she returns to Karisoke in June. She is appalled at how rundown her former home has become. She soon brings it back to its former glory, however, and vows never to leave again. Also in this year, her definitive book on her gorilla studies, *Gorillas in the Mist,* is released to worldwide acclaim.

1985 On the morning of December 27, Fossey is found murdered in her cabin.

1988 *Gorillas in the Mist,* the movie version of Fossey's life, is released, with Sigourney Weaver playing the lead role. The movie wins Golden Globe Awards for its musical score and for Weaver's performance.

To Find Out More

BOOKS

Fossey, Dian. *Gorillas in the Mist*. Boston, MA: Houghton Mifflin, 1983.

Freedman, Suzanne. *Dian Fossey: Befriending the Gorillas* (Innovative Minds Series). Austin, TX: Raintree/Steck Vaughn, 1997.

Matthews, Tom L. *Light Shining Through the Mist: A Photobiography of Dian Fossey*. Washington, D.C.: National Geographic, 1998.

Montgomery, Sy. *Walking With the Great Apes: Jane Goodall, Dian Fossey, Biruté Galdikas*. Boston, MA: Mariner Books, 1992.

Nadin, Corinne J., and Rose Blue. *Dian Fossey: At Home With the Giant Gorillas*. Brookfield, CT: Milbrook Press, 2002.

Schott, Jane A. *Dian Fossey and the Mountain Gorillas* (On My Own Biography Series). Minneapolis, MN: Carolrhoda Books, 2000.

Wood, Richard and Sara. *Dian Fossey*. Barrington, IL: Heinemann Library, 2001.

ORGANIZATIONS AND ONLINE SITES

Africa Online
http://africaonline.com/

This is a great site about all things African. It offers plenty of general information and lots of links. It contains everything from current political happenings to interactive maps and online discussion forums. It is ideal for learning about the continent and keeping up with what's going on there.

The Dian Fossey Gorilla Fund International
800 Cherokee Avenue, SE
Atlanta, Georgia 30315
1-800-851-0203
http://www.gorillafund.com/

This site contains information about Fossey's gorilla fund, plus recent news about the mountain gorillas and some Fossey-related matters. It has some interesting information about Fossey's life as well as information about the day-to-day life of gorillas.

GreenLeap
http://www.greenleap.com/

This is a fun and colorful site for kids containing all sorts of animal-related information, from conservation information to basic facts about many wild creatures. It includes news updates, polls, quizzes, and e-cards to send to friends. It is perfect for digging up information while doing reports.

The Jane Goodall Institute
http://www.janegoodall.org/

This is the home page for Goodall's institute, whose mission is to encourage others to protect the environments of all living things. It includes information on Goodall's life and current projects, the chimpanzees she has spent her life studying, how you can help the institute, and lots more.

The Leakey Foundation
http://www.leakeyfoundation.org/

This is the home page for the foundation Louis Leakey created in 1968 to further the study of human evolution. The site contains information on related news stories, current projects the organization sponsors, travel opportunities, and educational resources. It also has some history on Leakey and his family.

National Geographic Online
http://www.nationalgeographic.org/

The National Geographic Society has an excellent Web site with a variety of features, including interactive games, educational cartoons, breathtaking photographs, and lots more.

World Wildlife Fund
http://www.wwfus.org/

This is site for the U.S. branch of the World Wildlife Fund, which is one of the oldest and most respected conservation organizations. The site features links for kids, teachers, or just plain wildlife lovers. It has specific information on gorillas and other endangered species.

A Note on Sources

Much has been written about the intriguing life of Dian Fossey. Unfortunately, a certain percentage of it comes either from unreliable sources or from firsthand accounts of people who knew her that conflict with the accounts of others who knew her. Information on her antagonistic relationship with poachers, for example, was especially tricky to evaluate, as so many stories have been told that are closer to myth and legend than to the truth. To this end, I was forced to minimize coverage of this topic and include only what I judged to be factual.

The best source of information about the gorillas, of course, was Fossey herself. If not for her exhaustive work, *Gorillas in the Mist*, I would have had little to work with. Two other books that proved immensely helpful and enlightening were Hayes's *The Dark Romance of Dian Fossey* (which offered plenty of insight into Fossey's personality), and Mowat's *Virunga: The Passion of Dian Fossey*. As always, I relied on various Internet sources as well (too numerous to count), and, in a pinch, I could turn to Microsoft's excellent Encarta program for some quick fact-checking.

All in all, writing this book was a great experience and a true pleasure. As a longtime animal advocate and lover of all things wild and natural, I found tremendous inspiration in the story of this brave and determined person. I hope you enjoy reading it as much as I enjoyed creating it.

—*Wil Mara*

Index

About the Author

Wil Mara has been writing since the 1980s and has more than sixty books to his credit. Most of his early works were nonfiction titles about animals. In the early 1990s, he turned to fiction, ghostwriting three of the popular Boxcar Children Mysteries. He has since published four other novels, a handful of short stories, and numerous early-reader biographies for Scholastic Library Publishing. He lives with his wife and three daughters in northern New Jersey.